YAMTARAWALA

BLURB

The thematic concern of *Yamtarawala, the Warrior King* embraces man's purpose in the journey of aspirations and self fulfilment. Wanting to attain his long lost desire of kingship, Yamtarawala sets out conquering kingdoms and overcoming obstacles, even through deviant means. *Yamtarawala, the Warrior King* is a total drama with gripping plot structure heightened with suspense. The rich infusion of songs, music and dance in its dramatic action makes the play a lively theatrical piece. It is insightful, educative, and engaging with simple language and audience friendly
– **Prof Sunnie Ododo**, *FNAL, General Manager/CEO, National Theatre of Nigeria*

Akubuiro's dramatic rehistoricisation of the warrior-myth of the Kanem-Bornu Empire in *Yamtarawala, the Warrior King* is an audacious attempt to find answers to the many questions about historical warriorism and contemporary horror of terrorism. Ostensibly, the play suggests that the seeming invincibility of terrorist architecture across the land is a demonstration that our society is bereaved of archetypal warriors typified by Yamtarawala

– **Dr Abba Abba**, *DAAD and AHP Fellow and winner, NLNG Prize for Literary Criticism*

This play is epic, roundly captivating and intriguing. The quest for power and the extent to which an individual could go to attain it is the major ethos of this work –a quest that man lives with. Though the end of the central character is tragic, one cannot ignore his courage and the strength of his vision in the face of many discombobulations. In an amazing manner, Henry Akubuiro has succeeded in giving life to a historical tale, bringing it to function in the 21st century theatre. This brings to completion the multi-talentedness of the author to fit-in, and navigate all genres of literature with great ease and power

– **BM Dzukogi**, *Founder, Hilltop Art Centre, Minna*

In *Yamtarawala, the Warrior King*, Akubuiro dramatises a conundrum of intrigues between two princes in a contest for an empire. It is a drama of defiance and self-promotion that is beautifully told. The dialogue is simple and the play is laced with a good deal of spectacle and action that is skillfully handled with much sensitivity to the history and culture of Biu people

– **Shaibu Husseini**, *Ph.D, Director of Dance and Music, National Troupe of Nigeria*

This is a fast paced tragedy, an educative and riveting story that instantly invokes frames in the mind of the photographer, movements in space and time for the adventurous director, a desirable challenge for scenic designers and costumiers, and joy for thespians made of sterner stuff. A great historical recall.

– **Sobifaa Dokubo**, *veteran thespian, National Troupe of Nigeria.*

YAMTARAWALA
THE WARRIOR KING

A PLAY

HENRY AKUBUIRO

an imprint of
Abibiman Publishing

New York & London

Published in the United Kingdom in 2023 by Fabula/Plays,
an imprint of Abibiman Publishing.

Copyright © 2023 Henry Akubuiro

All rights reserved.
No part of this book may be reproduced, stored in a retrieval system, or transmitted in any form or by any means without permission in writing from the publisher.

Abibiman Publishing is registered under Hudics LLC in the United States and in the United Kingdom.

ISBN: 978-1-7392767-7-5

This is a work of fiction. Names, characters, places, and incidents either are the product of the author's imagination or are used fictitiously. Any resemblance to actual persons, living or dead, events, or locales is entirely coincidental.

Cover design by Stephen Embleton

Printed in the United Kingdom by Clays Ltd

DEDICATION

This work is dedicated to the octogenarian, Dr. Bukar Usman, President, Nigerian Folklore Society, whose amazing recollections of the ancient past and folklore of his Biu people of Borno State, inspired me to write this drama. Without his books, I wouldn't have visited Biu or have enough intellectual resources to embark on this creative project.

I also acknowledge the love shown by the Emir of Biu, Umar Mustapha Umar II, who welcomed me to his palace in December, 2022, allowing me to have a glimpse of some archival and cultural materials of his Bura people within and outside his palace during my second visit to the emirate.

I would like to thank my drama teacher at Imo State University, Owerri, Professor Isidore Diala, under whose guidance I wrote my B.A. dissertation on the drama of Esiaba Irobi and whose play, The Pyre, inspired me to write my first set of drama scripts.

I would also like to thank my darling wife, Mercy Akubuiro, who kept asking me, "When are you going to finish writing this book?" Those queries led to the cystilisation of this project.

I also wish to recognise Dr. Shauibu Hussein, Director of Dance and Music, National Troupe of Nigeria, who always invited me each time there was a play or performance by the National Troupe of Nigeria at the National Theatre. Those practical experiences watching the stage have offered me the lens of a dramaturg.

The same gratitude goes to the ace thespian, Dokubo Soibifa of the National Troupe of Nigeria, whose brilliance on stage as narrator/thespian in epic performances by the National Troupe of Nigeria have added zest to my thespian craft.

CAST

Abdullahi/Yamtarawala — Prince of Ngazargamu/King of Biu

Umar — Prince of Ngazargamu

Asga — Queen of Ngazargamu/mother of Prince Umar and Prince Abdullahi

Marivirayhel – son of Yamtarawala

Pachang –son of Yamtarawala

Diriwala –son of Yamtarawala

Pihtum– son of Yamtarawala

Awa: Yamtarawala's daughter.

Purkwa —Yamtarawala's daughter.

Queen 2 – wife of Yamtarawala/ Queen of Biu

Madu –Head of Kingmakers

Midala —Palace guard 1

Sadiq —Palace guard 2

Kabiru: The marabout

Slave raider 1

Slave Raider 2

Kwatam Gambo —Princess of Miringa

Pintu —her aide

Princess of Diwar

Jaina – her slave

Stranger 1

Stranger 2

Stranger 3

Kingmakers

Galadima

Narrator

Courtiers

Soldiers/Royal Warriors

Children

PREMIERE

Yamtarawala, the Warrior King was first staged on January 28, 2023, at Rosy Arts Theatre, Owerri, Imo State, by the following cast and crew:

Abdullahi/Yamtarawala — Sylvester Nwokedi
Umar — Chidozie Chukwubuike
Asga — Deborah Uzomah
Marivirayhel – Valentine Onumajuru
Pachang – Chuma King
Diriwala – Mike Duru
Pihtum– Amaechi Muruako
Awa: Bianca Opara
Purkwa — Nemdi Ogechi
Queen 2 – Deborah Uzomah
Madu – Chukwuma Ibezute
Midala — Stanley Philas

Sadiq — Ethel Uzoh
Kabiru: Michael Chiwueze
Slave raider 1 – John Eze
Slave Raider 2 – Mike Duru
Kwatam Gambo — Deborah Uzomah
Pintu — Madonna Onwuka
Princess of Diwar – Deborah Uzomah
Jaina – Nemdi Ogechi
Galadima – Ebere Ukah
Narrator – Sobifaa Dokubo
Director – Davidson Iwunze
Technical Director – Leon Eke
Stage Manager – Joe Ken
Sounds/Lights/Set design – Options Media
Costumiere: Umar Midala

PREFACE

The idea for this book first came to me in 2015 after reading *The History of Biu*, written by Dr. Bukar Usman, President, Nigerian Folklore Society, and coming across a brief, historical account on Yamtarawala, the Kanuri prince and warrior, who left Ngazargamu, the old capital of Kanem-Bornu Empire, on an empire-seeking adventure to Biu area in the 16th century. It was surprising to me there was no known drama recreating the battles and intrigues that trailed the Yamtarawala quest.

My interest for this dramatic pursuit also grew after my first ever visit to Biu Emirate in 2016 at a time Boko Haram was still claiming swathes of territories in Borno State, as my guide took me to Viukuthla village, the ancient capital of Biu, where

Yamtarawa also used to go for hunting centuries ago and also the burial place of Biu kings, spanning over 500 years, among other places of interest. I also saw the spot where Yamtarawala was reported to have sunk to the ground in Biu in a fit of rage and disillusionment.

Yamtarawala, lest we forget, is a celebrated mythical personage in Biu civilisation. Slightly different versions of his exploits from Ngazargamu to the Biu area exist, but this historical drama is a product of research.

This drama goes back to the sixteenth century and relives a major implosion in the Kanem-Bornu Empire caused by a kingship tussle and the departure of Yamtarawala and his 72 loyalists in an empire-seeking adventure to Biu area –the emirate, which is, presently, the second largest in Borno State.

In contemporary times, Biu is the only emirate in Borno that has failed to succumb to Boko Haram forays and the only emirate whose emir never fled during the stormy days of Boko Haram insurgency, till date.

In 2022, I embarked on another trip to Biu, visiting, among other places, the palace of the emir of Biu for a first-hand cultural experience of the Bura people, for a writer writing a historical work also needs that familiarity with the source of the narrative.

Yamtarawala, the Warrior King, is, thus, a drama that revisits ancient African past, wars, slavery and an archetypal hero's fall from grace to grass, while also interrogating a patrilineal society's matrix and exploitation of womanhood in the 16th century northeastern Nigerian society. It sheds light, too, on how one of Nigeria's least known but important ancient empires – Biu – was formed and the zeitgeist of that era.

Above all, the work re-examines the theory of consequentialism and the Machiavellian philosophy of the ends justify the means –how the quest for power in modern politics plays out with incredible intrigues, hubristic belief, as well as self-immolation as a last-gasp act and the futility of power. It beams light on leadership and hamartia.

While retaining the historical essence of the original tale, I have taken liberties in characterisation and dialogues by infusing dramatic elements that can enhance the performance. Covering live theatre as an arts and culture journalist for over a decade, including those by the National Troupe of Nigeria, has broadened my horizon on African theatrical traditions. With it comes a great awareness of content, spectacle and stagecraft.

Where the historical context of the original Yamtarawala story differs in this drama, I am just being a creative writer whose imagination is governed by afflatus. Here is something fresh in Nigerian drama from an exotic culture.

Henry Akubuiro,
Lagos, December, 2022.

PROLOGUE

(*A battlefield around the palace of the embattled Yemeni king. In the background acoustics, sounds of muskets reverberate and the stage lighting and mood reflect a tensed atmosphere.*

Confused voices echo. Cries of despair. Sounds of guns. Hooves and whinnies of running horses in a battlefield. Clashes of swords. Screams of the wounded. Sounds of burning houses.

On stage now, a number of masked men with pale skin appear with burnfire, singing mocking and victorious chants. They disappear after a couple of minutes.

In a short while, a frightened woman appears on stage, shaking, panting and in hiding, with fear written all over her face).

Asga: *(Exclaiming in Arabic, in fear). Taejab alkhawf! Taejab alkhawf!* They have killed my husband. My husband is gone. They have killed my hero. Who else do I have in this world? What else do I have left? Life has lost its meaning to me. Who will assuage my fears and lend me a helping hand? Who? Who? The Egyptian invaders have overrun our kingdom. They have overrun our palace. Where do I go now? Where? I have lost everything –my family, my home, my jewellery and my sanity. Where? Where? Where do I go now?

(Two blustering men with antiquated guns and chains enter the stage, searching here and there for a woman they heard her footfalls and discovering the harassed looking lady crouching in a corner).

Slave Raider 1: *(Laughing mechanically and pointing to Asga).* What good luck we got here! What a good catch!

Slave Raider 2: *(Smiling smugly).* What a beautiful day it's turning out to be. She must surely be a gift from our ancestors and Allah. And she fell into our hands without us running and gasping for breath or bruising our feet in hot pursuit.

Slave Raider 1: This is my definition of good fortune —that which is staring us in the face right now. Wow!

Slave Raider 2: How I wish everyday was like this.

Asga: (*On her knees, begging*). Please, don't harm me, Please, spare my life. They have already killed my husband. The Egyptians have killed the love of my life. Please, don't harm me. Please, please —

Slave Raider 1: Woman, we are not interested in your death. We are no hirelings from Pharaoh. We are not from the vanquished Yemen either. We come from Ngazargamu in the great Kanem-Bornu Empire. We are like birds in the sky; we roam wherever our might and horses allow us to go.

Slave Raider 2: (*To Asga*). So, you are more useful to us alive than dead.

Asga: (*Gasping*). I curse my luck! (*Exclaiming in anguish*). *Taejab alkarb!* (*She struggles frantically and screaming as Slave Raider 1 lifts her off her feet and off the stage*). *Atrukni wahdi!* Leave me alone! *Atrukni wahdi!* Leave me alone! *Atrukni wahdi!* Leave me alone!

Slave Raider 2: (*As he departs the stage with the chains*). That's a good catch. We are riding our luck. Our cowries from Ngazargamu are bound to multiply overnight *(laughs aloud)*. What a good day! (*To the audience*). Aren't we lucky?

(*Sounds of running hooves and whinnies of horses echo and trail off in the background acoustics*).

Narrator: (*Appears on stage*). Lend me your ears, everybody. I want to take you back to the 16th century and tell you about Yamtarawala, the son of the king of Ngazargamu, the ancient capital of Kanem-Bornu Empire, whose mother came from Yemen.

Yamtarawala's mother, Asga, was a beautiful slave put up for sale in a slave market. The son of the Yemeni king saw her and liked her, and bought her. But when he presented her to his father as the girl he would like to marry, the king snatched her, and she became the king's wife.

It wasn't long before the king of Egypt attacked Yemen, putting the kingdom into disarray. Queen Asga escaped and wandered into the bush from where she was captured by the roving slave hunters of the king of Ngazargamu, Kanem-Bornu, who brought her to the palace of Ngazargamu.

On seeing her, the king of Ngazargamu remembered what his marabout had earlier told him that he was going to marry a slave girl, and decided to marry her as a second wife (his first wife had no issue).

Before long, the new wife announced to the king she was pregnant, and the king was overjoyed; but the king's bodyguards and courtiers suspected she must have been impregnated in Yemen before her arrival in Ngazargamu, but they didn't want to tell the king to incur his wrath. So the new wife bore a son named Abdullahi, who was to become Yamtarawala, and the second son, Umar. The two lookalike princes lived together peacefully with their parents until the king of Ngazargamu died. Which of the two princes will be the new king of Ngazargamu? There is tension in the land.

PART 1

SCENE 1

(Early 16th century. The king's palace, Ngazargamu, capital of Kanem-Bornu Empire. Carvings and drums hang on the walls. A mournful song plays out by the Chorus, lamenting the passage of the king. On stage, the Kingmakers, all seated on mats, wearing sorrowful visages, shake their heads. A meeting is about to commence on how to select a new king. The dirge slowly fades away as the leader of the Kingmakers, Madu, rises up, momentarily pacing about on stage before facing his colleagues).

Madu: *(Greeting). Assalamu Alaikum.*

Kingmakers: *Wa alaikum assalam.*

Madu: It's been three days since our great leader joined his ancestors and was led to rest. We have cried our hearts out. Esteemed Kingmakers of Ngazargamu, tears have fallen from our eyes like rain gurgling down to the Ngazargamu River. For hours, our eyelids have swollen up like the pyramid of Giza. We have given up joy, draped in grief (*shaking his head*) all because our revered monarch is no more. Our voices have become hoarse from crying like the slacken cords of a loose guitar. May Allah accept his soul in Ajami.

Kingmakers: (*In unison*). Amin.

Madu: *Alhamdulillah*. Praise be to Allah. But our deluge of tears won't bring back the dead; it won't bring back our lovely monarch. Kingmakers of Ngazargamu, time is of essence. It's time to play our customary role — appointing a new king. As tradition demands, we are going to crown one of the two sons of the king. This means, according to our age-long tradition, the eldest, Abdullahi, isn't it?

Kingmakers: (*In unison*). It is! (*The late king's guards who are standing at both ends of the stage, fully kitted with swords, and a few courtiers around, break into murmurs of discontent, shaking their heads in faint protest*).

Madu: (*Addressing them*). Quiet there! Guards, your presence in this palace doesn't include performing an oversight function. Why are you interrupting me? Has morality taken flight from your senses? (*Turning to the Kingmakers*) The death of the king doesn't mean respect doesn't exist anymore in Ngazargamu. No! Kingmakers of Ngazargamu, it is our bounden duty to present the next king to the good people of Ngazargamu and the entire Kanem-Bornu Empire. Our ancestors have made us a beacon of hope when a pall of darkness falls on the throne of Ngazargamu. We have to invite Abdullahi and inform him of our collective decision to be our new king and plan the ceremony without wasting time, am I in order?

Kingmakers: Yes, that's our tradition (*the guards shake their heads again, grumbling*).

Madu: (*Angrily addressing the palace guards*). Why are you still murmuring after my first warning? Oh, you want to be the new king? (*The Kingmakers burst into derisive laughter, as the leader of the palace guards raises up his hand languorously to speak*).

Midala: Sorry, if you misunderstand my reaction. There is nothing like that. I have no ambition to be a king, for it's a tall order for a mere palace guard like me; the stool of kingship doesn't run in my ancestry. But I have something important to say. Please, permit me to share a secret with you. If I don't say it now, posterity won't forgive me. I don't want to offend this great empire and the ancestors of Ngazargamu by playing the coward when the circumstance on ground demands the contrary.

Madu: *(Switching his gaze to the bewildered Kingmakers).* Do we permit this clown to speak in this eminent gathering? Do jesters now talk when Kingmakers of Ngazargamu are having an important discussion? Do we allow Midala to air his view?

Kingmakers *(Nodding their heads, anxious to hear from the guard).*

Kingmaker 2: Let's allow him, please. Sometimes one may find wisdom in foolish things said by a jester. Even a mad man can speak the truth sometimes.

Madu: *(To Midala).* You can speak, the clownish palace guard, but never bore us with a cock and bull story. The solemnity of this occasion doesn't call for trifles. The king is no more, but we still have the authority to take prisoners.

Midala: For more than two decades, my colleagues and I who served the late king have kept this secret to ourselves, but we don't want to go to our graves with suffocating guilt —

Madu: (*Listening with mouth agape*). What secret are you talking about, clown?

Kingmakers: (*Looking at each other*). What secret?

Midala: We were at this palace when Queen Asga arrived as the second wife of the king twenty-three years ago. Everybody was happy when she bore the first child, but we know that child doesn't belong to the king —

Madu: Abominable talk! What nonsense are you saying, Midala? (*Moving to grab him by the throat*). Why have you chosen this time to rubbish the queen of Ngazargamu?

Kingmakers (*Rising to restrain him*). Let's allow the jester to say his mind.

Midala: Sorry if this revelation offends you, but I stand for the truth, and I will always say nothing but the truth —

Sadiq: *(Corroborating)*. Midala said nothing but the truth. We were serving the king dutifully when the queen arrived here, but she was in the early days of her pregnancy then, from all the signs we could see. We noticed certain strangeness about her pregnant condition, but the king didn't seem to have noticed anything.

Midala: By our calculation, she gave birth to Prince Abdullahi in her seventh month as the queen —

Sadiq: Which means she was already pregnant from Yemen, carrying the child of the king of Yemen, for we were told she fled Yemen when her husband was killed by the Egyptian army. The slave raiders of the king who brought her here are closely related to me (*Kingmakers stare at each other in bewilderment*).

Midala: We didn't want to tell the king of that bitter truth, because he was overjoyed with the arrival of the new baby, his first offspring ever—

Sadiq: And our lives would have been at risk, too, if we dared open that can of worms.

Midala: Therefore, we are afraid, if you go ahead and crown Abdullahi the new king of Ngazargamu, our ancestors won't forgive all of us —

Sadiq: For it's a sacrilege in our culture for a stranger to be crowned the king of Ngazargamu. It hasn't happened before (*Kingmakers fold their hands in total shock, exchanging glances*), and this won't be the first, unless we want to set a bad precedent.

Madu: (*After recovering from the shock*) I said it! Clowns are not given the mandate to speak in a gathering of Kingmakers. I said it! I am tempted to dismiss this story as a tale by moonlight told by a grandmother in the silence of the night, but this is an allegation we can't take lightly. We can feel its weight (*shudders*), even when it sounds more like the tale of someone with the calling of a jester.

Look, if we blindly crown a new king without getting to the roots of this matter, the consequences would be upon not only us but the entire Ngazargamu and Kanem-Bornu! We have found ourselves in a dilemma, but it's not a difficult one to solve. Kingmakers of Ngazargamu, let's send one of the courtiers to the dusty alley of Ngazargamu to consult Kabiru, the all-knowing marabout, to tell us the way forward. Some things are simply beyond human comprehension, you know. I am sure he will tell us how we can bail ourselves out of this quagmire.

(*Light fades as they disperse*).

SCENE 2

(The king's palace, Ngazargamu. Assorted drums, skulls of lions and other wild animals hang on the walls, as well as a cage of parrots. A dirge echoes from the Chorus, lamenting the death of the king. Two cows are tied to a stake, mowing. Kingmakers are joined on the right side of the stage by the two princes of Ngazargamu – Abdullahi and Umar – and the queen. A group of people, constituting the citizens of Ngazargamu, sit by the left side of the stage. Madu, the head of the Kingmakers, dressed in kukwa — a long, roomy, heavily embroidered garment — with a red cap, steps up to address the crowd).

Madu: *(Greeting).* Assalamu Alaikum.

All: Wa alaikum assalam.

Madu: The good people of Ngazargamu, I greet you all. Alhamdulillahi. Days ago, our dear king went to the great beyond. We have no doubt he has gone to Ajami. We are proud of his achievements. He served this great empire well. We have all cried a river of tears, and sadness has engraved itself on our hearts, but today is a new dawn. We will be finding out who's the leader of this vast empire.

Kingmaker 2: When our ordinary eyes can't see what's hidden in the spiritual realm, we call upon the marabout to tell us the will of Allah.

Kingmaker 3: And the great Kabiru from the dusky alley of Ngazargamu has spoken the will of Allah —that each of the two sons should be given a cow to slaughter.

Kingmaker 4: And how each of them slaughters the cow will determine who becomes the new king (*the crowd chatters excitedly, divided who among the two princes may slaughter the cow better*).

Madu: Alhamdulillah. The die is cast, the good people of Ngazargamu. On the surface, this is a simple test for both of you (*pointing at the seated princes*), but it's also a difficult test to pass. How deft you are in killing your cow will elevate you to that exalted throne (*pointing at the unoccupied golden throne with a crown on the seat*), the hallowed throne of Ngazargamu and its vast empire (*spreading his arms wide and looking into the sky*).

Today, the blue sky is wearing an apron, and I can see the clouds floating pass in wonder. The heavens are fully behind us. We are the descendants of the legendary Mai Ali Gazi, the founder of the great Kanem-Bornu Empire. Our empire stretches from the fork of the Komadugu Gana River to Komadugu Yobe. Ngazargamu has always been a great place, and it will remain great from generation to generation.

(*Turning to Abdullahi*). We now call on the first son, Abdullahi, to step forward and grab the machete to perform the first task. He has to show us why he deserves to be the king of this great empire.

Abdullahi: (*Greeting*). Assalamu Alaikum.

All: Wa alaikum assalam.

Abdullahi: (*Grabbing the machete and hitting the back of his chest with arrogance, in a show of might*). I am Abdullahi, the terror of the lions and hyenas of Mandara Mountains. At 16, I chased a pack of hyenas alone to the mountains until they disappeared from view. At 18, I killed my first lion. Since then, I have brought many heads of lions as trophies to this great palace *(the crowd claps for him)*. Killing a mere cow without claws is like the simplest of tasks to perform for a warrior. I prefer stronger challenges meant for real men *(he pulls the cow down and slaughters it with ease. The crowd roars in delight as he steps back to sit on the mat)*.

Madu: *(Beckoning on Umar)*. It's now your turn to step forward and perform your task. Show us why you deserve to be the king.

Umar: Assalamu Alaikum.

All: Wa alaikum assalam.

Umar: *(Rising solemnly and laughing quizzically)*. I am a man of few words, but my actions speak louder than the loudest of voices. When the drums beat at the market square, its echoes reach different corners of the community. I am like the hyena that takes away the treasure trove of the lion caught with difficulties without a fight. I am Umar –my strength is in my vault of wisdom. *(Turning to Kingmakers)*. I call upon you to join me in this task, because killing a royal cow is not the duty of one man. My father taught me well *(Abdullahi and the crowd burst into derisive laughter)*.

Kingmakers: (*Addressing Madu*). Are we permitted to join the prince to kill the cow?

Madu: (*Giggles*). Why not? His wish is our command. When a weakling struggles to climb a mountaintop, will you, as an elder, fold your hands and watch him tumble to the ground?

Umar: (*As Kingmakers pull the cow down*). Please, help me to face the head of the cow eastward (*Umar holds the cow by its torso and slaughters it, and murmurs of discontent rend the air from the crowd*).

Madu: Thank you, Prince Abdullahi and Prince Umar. We are proud of you two. Your mother, Queen Asga, who nurtured you to adulthood, will equally be proud of such talented young men (*the queen stands up to acknowledge cheers*). I call them the stallions of Ngazargamu. (*Addressing the crowd and the audience concurrently*). Today is a day of joy. It's a day willed by Allah to wipe away the tears of grieving men, women and children of Ngazargamu. We now call on Kabiru, the great marabout, to give us the verdict of Allah on this blessed day. Alhamdulillahi.

Kabiru: Assalamu Alaikum.

All: Wa alaikum assalam.

Kabiru: (*Holding his prayer beads, steps to the middle of the stage and utters prayers*). I am nothing but the messenger of Allah. I have no personal interest in whoever becomes the king, but only Allah makes a king (*silence falls*). Now, listen attentively, everybody: the cow of the king-to-be is not meant to be slaughtered by one man alone but with the assistance of others. Also, it should be killed with its head facing the east. Without equivocation, Kingmakers of Ngazargamu, the golden crown belongs to Umar (*the audience roars in delight, jumping up and down, except Abdullahi and his mother who are wearing frowning faces*).

Madu: (*Holding the crown*). Allah chooses a king, and not man. Allah has spoken, and it's our responsibility to do the will of Allah. Alhamdulillahi. (*Together with other Kingmakers, they walk Umar to the throne and place the crown on him, with a sword in his right hand*). The people of Ngazargamu, here is your new king (*the crowd roars and bows down to the new king, except Abdullahi, as elaborate festivity and dance, lasting for minutes, commence in celebration of the new king*).

Abdullahi: (*Silence falls as he rises to speak*). I can't believe my eyes. Today, I have seen justice denied. I have seen an unusual conspiracy against an innocent man. My inherited crown has been taken away from me. But I can't stand this daylight robbery. I can't bow down to Umar as my king – a boy I knew the day he was born; a boy I helped to learn how to take the first steps and say the first syllables. I won't stay here anymore to endure this show of shame. I am a child of destiny, born to be great. No man can stop the sun from shining. So I am leaving Ngazargamu with my last words: *Youman teram wallahianasultan, insha Allah* (one day, you will see that I am a chief, God willing). And I add to it: *Yau ma tara wal* (one day, we will meet again).

(*Yamtawarala storms out of the stage, furious, leaving everybody speechless. The crowd disperse*).

Narrator: (*Walks onto the stage*). Poor Abdullahi, he thought he was robbed of his right, but he was just a victim of circumstance. Until the king died, the queen never told him this secret – that she ran away from Yemen with the pregnancy of the Yemeni king before she was captured by the slave raiders of Ngazargamu. Till this day, she never told her first son that he was a stranger in Ngazargamu. But Abdullahi was the most popular of the two sons, and was destined to be great. He didn't want to play second fiddle to the new king, so he raided the armoury of the king and carted away weapons. With 72 loyalists he convinced to follow him, he fled Ngazargamu without knowing his exact destination, but he was determined to found a new empire where he would reign supreme.

SCENE 1

(Semi darkness prevails on stage, showing figures carrying loads and weapons, wandering in the forest, amid the noises of camels, horses and goats in the background acoustics, plus humans ordering the animals to keep moving.

Some women among them complain of journey weariness, and beg their leader to rest for a while before continuing the journey. Thereafter, silence falls. When the light appears, the stage shows tired people either sitting on the floor or lying on the floor. Four palanquin bearers are seen carrying Yamtarawala to the stage).

Yamtarawala: (*Ordering the palanquin bearers*). Put me down, please. (*A momentary pause*). I am proud of everybody for answering my call to embark on this journey. You are the chosen ones. For many days, we have been on the road, trekking to meet our destinies. We have left our beautiful homes, courtyards, cows, horses, stallions, camels and oxen behind. We have left our barns, our friends and relatives behind. We have left many goats behind, because we couldn't take them all with us.

We have left behind some of our precious ornaments —gold, silver and bronze — behind, because our bags couldn't contain them all at the same time. But, frankly, we have lost nothing. Soon we will gain everything, and many more.

As you sit and lie down in dejection, I feel your pains. I consider it the height of self-sacrifice. You have left the comfort of Ngazargamu to follow me on this perilous journey, but it wasn't a bad decision. How long can we remain in a kingdom where injustice prevails? How can we stay back and grovel on the feet of Prince Umar with his illegal ascension to the throne of Mai Ngazargamu? You are all brave in your decision to reject the Ngazargamu charade. History will be kind to you all.

Our journey to freedom has just started. Our journey to greatness has just started. Generations unborn will hear this story. When I left Ngazargamu, I left a message to the usurpers at the palace: *"Youman teram wallahianasultan, insha Allah"*, and I mean every word of it.

I have seen the vision of what the future looks like, a very beautiful place, a fertile land, a land of flowing rivers, rocks and mountains; but I don't know where it is in reality. But the path to this haven of peace is not going to be too smooth. I don't mean to scare you, for we will surely overcome. We have brought with us some of the best armoury Ngazargamu could boast of and some of the best calvary men, Moroccan muskets, swords, battle-axes, broad-bladed spears, body armour, poisoned wooden arrows, daggers, among others.

We have brought with us some of the best loyal fighters from the army of Ngazargamu. We may not be too many, but our strength is in our finesse. Make no mistake about it: obstacles will come our way, but we will suffer no villains gladly. We will crush any hindrance on our way, insha Allah. I, therefore, bank on your cooperation. We are not up to 100 men and women, but we are a strong army. As we take chiefdoms and settlements along the way, our community will grow and our army will expand. I want everybody to stand now *(they all stand up)*.

The journey ahead, as I said earlier, isn't going to be an easy one, but we can make it a walkover if we are determined. In this regard, I am going to make some important announcements. I want to appoint a few men who will work with me temporarily, for we don't have our own empire yet. I will serve as your leader and also the leader of the army. I will be appointing Yusuf as the Galadima, leader of the army (*a dark, muscular man appears to his right*). You will be assisting me as the commander of the army. I have known you since I was born, a strong man, who has never been beaten in a wrestling contest. You have been part of the Ngazargamu army for a while, and you have shared in the glory of our recent successes in battlefields. You are a man with uncommon will power, very reliable and important to our empire-seeking adventure as we head towards the Mandara Mountains (*everybody claps for him as he bows down to Yamtarawala*).

Galadima: I thank you, our great leader. It's my honour to serve our people. I promise you I won't disappoint. Mother bird doesn't abandon her tender chicks, because guiding them is a task that must be done.

Yamtarawala: I believe in your ability and I trust your words (*looking around*). You will be training the army if I am not available for whatever reason. Also, we need entertainers, for when our spirit is low, we need music to rouse us up. We also need courtiers who will be working with me as special advisers (*volunteers raise up their hands*). I thank you all for identifying with our struggle for freedom; our determination to build a new empire. History will not forget your sacrifices.

Now, I want everybody to go and rest. When we wake up tomorrow, we need to make ourselves happy with Bansuwe dance. We will continue to make ourselves happy, for in front of us are many unhappy people, who won't be willing to let us get to our destination with ease. They will converge to stop us, but we are unstoppable. They will conspire to make us unhappy, but smiles will never elude our faces. They will move to break our ranks, but we are one formidable force that will never falter in our resolve. The echoes of our happiness will reach the boundaries of Ngazargamu, Bulala, Yemen, Sudan, Egypt, Ethiopia, Arabia and beyond. Thank you. Thank you. Thank you, all.

SCENE 2

(*The moment the palanquin bearers carrying Yamtarawala walk onto the stage and drop him gently on the platform, he springs to his feet and takes a seat. A group of male dancers appear on stage, and frenetic drumming and dancing rend the air, winning the admiration of Yamtarawala, who nods away in delight. The Bansuwe dance lasts for minutes before they leave the stage, paving way for soldiers to perform their war dance. At the end of the dance, Yamtarawala addresses the crowd*).

Yamtarawala: Galadima!

Galadima: The supreme commander. *(Greeting)*. Assalamu Alaikum.

Yamtarawala: Wa alaikum assalam.

Yamatarawala: (*Standing on his feet*). I am delighted by the performance of your men. I am equally impressed with that of the first set of dancers before them. At every point in time, we should be in high spirits (*walking around and inspecting the soldiers*). We are on the way to becoming the strongest army in the world. Kanem-Bornu will hear our success story and quake at what we have achieved within a short time, insha Allah.

(*Returns to Galadima*). Prepare everybody. Tomorrow, we move to Limbur village. From there, we head towards Gujba. I am expecting a resistance from that point. But I trust my men. The locals don't have the kind of weapons we have, so I don't expect them to stop our movement, no matter how hard they may try.

Working with my father has made me understand the strengths and weaknesses of the neighbouring communities. We fear no foe. They should be the ones afraid of us. We are a strong army with weapons carted away from Ngazargamu — weapons sourced from as far as Egypt, Morocco, Ethiopia, Arabia and Ottoman. We fear no foe. Thank you. Thank you. Thank you, all (*he leaves the stage, and others follow behind*).

Narrator: (*Enters the stage*). Yamtarawala and his adventurers proceeded to Limbur, and were warmly received by the villagers. Everybody knew him as the prince of Ngazargamu. He settled here for a while, while planning how to conquer unfriendly settlements ahead. As expected, his spies had returned to give him reports that those settlements wouldn't allow them to enter their territories without a fight. Yamtarawala was expecting that news, but he didn't panic.

With his superior weapons, his men, together with those he conscripted from Limbur, fought and overwhelmed several settlements after Gujba who stood in their way. When he got to Mandaragrua, he faced stiff opposition, for Mandaragrua had never been defeated in a war before his arrival.

SCENE 3

(*A battlefield. Two armies appear on stage facing each other. One is Yamtarawala's army and the other is the Mandaragrua army. Yamtarawala's army looks more sophisticated and better armed. Surprisingly, the ragtag army of Mandaragrua refuses to be intimidated to surrender.*

A fight breaks out among the two camps. Yamtarawala is locked with the leader of the other army in a fierce sword combat, and fails to get the upper hand. Galadima, who is also fighting with a strong Mandaragrua opponent, fails to overpower him with his sword.

For about five minutes, the two armies keep fighting to break each other down as gun fires and clash of swords resonate. Eventually, Yamtarawala's army is forced to retreat by the enemies, who dance away in celebration).

Narrator: (*Re-enters the stage*). As you can see, Yamtarawala didn't have his way at Mandaragrua. The chiefdom had a strong juju made with horn. Whenever there was a war, they would bury the horn in a refuse dump, and they would always win.

To overcome this obstacle, Yamtarawala connived with one of his hunters to befriend one of the princesses of Mandaragrua. The relationship blossomed and led to marriage. Yamtarawala and his team were patient until children began to come into the marriage, after which he told the princess that, if they could get the hidden horn, her children would reign sooner than later. She agreed and fetched the elusive horn to Yamtarawala.

PART 3

SCENE 1

(An open field. Yamtarawala appears on stage with a group of excited soldiers. He is holding the elusive, sacred horn of Mandaragrua, having deceived the princess to lead him to the where the hidden horn was kept. As he raises the sacred horn up, everybody stretches their necks to have a glimpse of the charm that prevented them from defeating the Mandaragrua army).

Yamtarawala: *(Laughing in derision).* At last, we have the sacred horn tormenting us.

All: Yeah! Yeah!

Yamtarawala: Let's congratulate ourselves (*everybody raises their fists in the* air).

Galadima: I have no doubt in your ability to solve this mystery. You are a leader who combines brain with brawl. The sacred horn in your hands is another indication that, to get what you want, you use what you have. Great leader, you have that charm to disarm beauties.

Yamtarawala: *(Laughing)*. What surprised me most was that the princess of Mandaragrua thought I loved her. Poor woman, she never knew I was after the horn, not her heart.

Galadima: I pity her also. To mount a horse and embark on a long ride is filled with so much fun and pleasant memories. When you dismount from the horse, it's no longer the same fun. This, I guess, is how the princess feels now.

Yamtarawala: Our greatest joy now is getting this sacred horn. It makes our victory assured and our journey to our destination one step closer. A broken heart heels with time, but if it doesn't heal with time, our sympathies go to the brokenhearted.

Galadima: You have spoken well.

Yamtarawala: For now, let's savour this precious moment. We have done our best to lessen our burden, but, as we rejoice, let's remember that Mandaragrua hasn't fallen yet.

Galadima: That's the reason we won't let this momentary triumph get into our heads. Let's go and rest and prepare for another battle with Mandaragrua.

Yamtarawala: You are right. Unlike the last time, we are going to come out, this time, victorious. I have no doubt in my mind we are going to carry the day, insha Allah.

(*They leave the stage in high spirits*).

Narrator: Yamtarawala's army made another charge and, this time, conquered Mandaragrua and some settlements after it. But the tough times are not over yet. Miringa, ahead of them, presents another formidable opposition, a place known for its legendary charm used in warding off adversaries.

SCENE 2

(The voices of the Chorus are heard in praise of Yamtawara's heroism. Soldiers enter the stage matching as the palanquin bearers follow in their wake, carrying Yamtarawala. When Yamtarawala alights, he smiles in self-contentment).

Yamtarawala: Assalamu Alaikum.

All: Wa alaikum assalam.

Yamtarawala: Let's congratulate ourselves, once again. We have come a long way from Ngazargamu. We have conquered territory after territory, taking along slaves. From less than 100 people who left Ngazargamu with me, we have grown into hundreds and some of us have even raised families. I believe we are walking in the right direction. I am sure, by now, the news of our exploits must have reached Ngazargamu, and all the chiefdoms that lay in front of us. When they hear that Yamtarawala, the prince of Ngazargamu, is coming (*everybody bursts into laughter*), they flee and hide in different corners (*demonstrating*). I am Yamta the great. What I promise is what I deliver (*everybody nods their heads*).

Galadima: (*Cheering him*). Yamta the great. Yamta the conqueror. Yamta, the alter ego of Mai Ngazargamu of blessed memory.

Yamtarawala: (*With shoulders held high*). I salute you. Tell me, what lies ahead of us.

Galadima: Miringa is the next settlement to take.

Yamtarawala: How strong is the army?

Galadima: It's an invincible army, as I am told.

Yamtarawala: (*Rebuking*). Stop! No army under the earth is totally invincible. It may appear to be invincible, because it has not met its match. No army is invincible to Yamta the great. My father told me how the invincible Bulala army conquered territory after territory from Libya to Kanembu area, down to Lake Chad. But it took Mai Idris Aloma to strategise and conquer the Bulala. Give me, Miringa, please.

Galadima: You haven't heard all the stories about Miringa yet.

Yamtarawala: Do they have Pharaoh's chariots?

Galadima: No!

Yamtarawala: Ottoman's howitzers?

Galadima: No.

Yamtarawala: Ethiopia's muskets?

Galadima: No!

Yamtarawala: Morocco's calvary?

Galadima: No.

Yamtarawala: Carthage mortar gunners?

Galadima: No.

Yamtarawala: Assyrian fighting elephants?

Galadima: No.

Yamtarawala: Arabian jinis?

Galadima: No.

Yamtarawala: Congo's warrior pygmies?

Galadima: No.

Yamtarawala: What, then?

Galadima: They have a strong juju.

Yamtarawala: Hu! Another juju. These infidels can never change their filthy ways with sorcery. They create different, mysterious objects and use its power to intimidate civilised people like us. This is ridiculous. At Mandaragrua, they used a mere horn to scare the hell out of us. This is ridiculous. These infidels are funny! Allah Akbar!

Galadima: Are you scared, Yamta?

Yamtarawala: Yamta the great can't be scared by ordinary objects made by infidels. Now tell me, what does this one at Miringa look like? A carved head of a hydra headed monster? A crocodile carving? A gigantic baobab tree with tied objects around it? How does it look?

Galadima: I haven't seen it, but the captured soldiers from Mandaragrua say it's called Mumba, a charm with the ability to ward off the strongest army in the world. It's hidden in a secret shrine called Tibal, from where it provides the people with spiritual defence.

Yamtarawala: Hu! You mean the Mumba is stronger than that of Mandaragrua which held us back for many days?

Galadima: So I heard.

Yamta: *(Shudders).* This is getting ridiculous. So preposterous.

Galadima: Are you scared of Mumba?

Yamtarawala: Allah Akbar! Yamta the great can't be terrified by an ordinary object created by man. No! Never! The Holy Koran, in Surah IV, verse 76, says: 'Believers fight for the cause of Allah, while disbelievers do battle for the cause of idols. So fight the minions of the devil'. And that's exactly what we want to do. Like Maduragua, Miringa will fall, insha Allah.

All: Allahu Akbar!

Yamtarawala: Yes, God is great. Victory songs will never vanish from our mouths until we get to our final destination. The journey is only half done. We will fight until we get to our final destination. Just last night, I saw, once again, the great land Allah has given us. It's a land surrounded by plateau, a fortress of rocks and mountains. It's also a land with lush forests for our farms —one full of animals for hunting. This land has a big lake coursing through it. It's a beautiful land for all of us, insha Allah. This is going to be our reward for stepping out of Ngazargamu. Lift up your spirits, warriors of this emerging empire; your reward is coming (*everybody claps in delight, and they break into a dance*).

SCENE 3

(*Yamtarawala is surrounded by eager children who have gathered to listen to a tale by moonlight. The stage is sparingly lit to reflect the moonlight setting in the midst of surrounding darkness. The children are seen joking among themselves, some pinching one another, while some laugh excitedly. In the background acoustics are chirps of insects and cries of birds to reflect the forest environment they are in. Armed guards are seen at different positions*).

Yamtarawala: (*Calls for calm, and the children obey*). Good evening, wonderful children.

Children: Good evening, great one.

Yamtarawala: Are you happy?

Children: Yes, we are.

Yamtawarala: You know what this time means?

Children: Yes, story time.

Yamtarawala: Thank you very much. Storytelling has been part of our culture right from time. We have left Ngazargamu, but we didn't leave our cultural heritage. Wherever we go, we go along with our culture. Tonight, you are going to hear a new story.

Children: *(In excitement).* Yeah! Tell us the story.

Yamtarawala: *(Smiling).* You are going to hear a beautiful story. I will call on one of us to tell you a story, in keeping with our tradition. Our elders have so many stories in their repository to tell us at every point in time. Great lessons abound in these stories.

(*Orders a guard to fetch Galadima*).

Galadima: (*Entering the stage*). I am here, great one.

Yamtarawala: The moon has peeped out from the sky, beaming with smiles. It's that time of the night when elders regale the young ones with our ancient tales. We don't have grey hairs, but we are like elders to These young ones. Folktales are our stories. They are our lives. They tell us how the circumstances of olden days shape today. Galadima, our children are eagerly waiting for you.

Galadima: *(To Children)*. Are you ready?

Children: Yes, we are ready.

Galadima: Now, lend me your ears. I am going to tell you a story about The Cat and the Unfaithful Rat. Are you ready?

Children: Yes, we are.

Galadima: *(A faint, steady flute plays in the background as the story begins. The scene may be acted out as a pantomime by kids dressed like animals).* Once upon a time, a cat and a rat became friends. They were so fond of each other that they decided to live together in the same house. They trusted and cared about each other.

As their relationship became stronger, the rat came up with a suggestion. "It is good to be wise and plan for the future," he began. "So, let's stock up a room in this house with food for the extremely cold and harsh harmattan season when food is usually scarce."

"That's a good idea," the cat said, in agreement. From that day, they began to stockpile food.

One day, the cat travelled to another town to witness the traditional naming ceremony of his sister's baby. In his absence, the rat headed for the harmattan stock and began to eat the food.

When the cat returned home, the rat did not tell him what she had done. Rather, to distract him, she kept asking, "What did your sister get, a male or a female child?"

"A task is only difficult before it is started," the cat responded.

After a few weeks, the cat travelled to rejoice with someone else whose child was being named.

The rat again sneaked in and ate more voraciously from the harmattan stock. When the cat returned, she welcomed him warmly and asked," What did the woman get, a male or a female."

"For today and tomorrow, nothing was left," the cat said.

On the cat's return from the third naming event, the rat, as usual, asked, "Was it a boy or a girl?"

The cat ignored the question again, and said, "It has happened and it has happened."

Soon after, another baby was to be named and the cat yet again travelled. When he returned from his fourth journey, the rat, more than ever before, pestered him, asking, "Is it a male or a female?"

Unknown to the cat, the rat had greedily and dishonestly eaten up their stockpile.

The cat, wearing a very stern look, yelled, "You talk too much and you are a troublemaker!" Thereupon, he pounced on the rat and ate her.

Yamtarawala: *(To Galadima)*. Thank you. Thank you. That's an interesting story, Galadima. *(To Children)*. Hope you are happy?

Children: Yes, we are, great one.

Yamtarawala: I am happy to hear this. Don't forget, every story has a moral, and the moral in the story is that unfaithfulness and dishonesty lead to destruction sooner or later.

It's time for you to go back to your parents. We will meet again for new stories. Thank you for coming.

Children: Thank you, great one.

(*The excited children leave the stage*).

Yamtarawala: (*Talking to himself*). Warriors do not entertain the fear of death before embarking on a war. Galadima has spoken of Mumba of Miringa and how previous invaders had fared badly. So, do we abandon our charge for Miringa because of ordinary juju? That would be cowardice. Cowardice doesn't run in the veins of the great Yamta. The bigger the obstacles, the stronger we get. (*Addressing Galadima*). Galadima!

Galadima: Great one, I am all ears.

Yamtarawala: Each time I see you, I see one of the greatest warriors in living memory. A humble legend. Each time I see you on the battlefield, you remind me of the lightly armed Songhay warriors who defeated the dreaded Moroccan caravan. When I see you take down giants, I am glad that we have a great warrior in our ranks like you. You are a treasure worth more than the treasure trove of Ethiopia (*Galadima takes a bow*).

Galadima: I am flattered, great one.

Yamta: You deserve all the praise.

Galadima: Thank you, great one.

Yamtarawala: (*Paces up and down*). Miringa is there for the taking. Miringa stands between us and greatness, how prepared are we to overcome the enemy?

Galadima: Great one, our warriors are always prepared to take on any foe. We have demonstrated this in the last few years. We have been on the scorching roads and mountains. We have overrun chiefdoms and settlements that have stood in our way. We have spared no ebullient chief and we have taken hundreds of prisoners, who have joined our formidable fighting force. Great one, we are always prepared, ready to be in the match again.

Yamtarawala: I love those powerful words by a man of candour. Warriors are known for matching their words with action. It's time for us to move again, westward to Miringa. Prepare the army. Alert our people. We won't stop matching until we get to our final destination. History is not made by cowards; it is made by brave men and men with visions and the drive to actualise them. That's what distinguishes us from ordinary mortals. History will be fair to all of us, insha Allah (they *leave the stage, with Yamtarawala carried by the palanquin bearers*).

PART 4

SCENE 1

(*The voices of the Chorus and drumming come alive in praise of the heroism of Yamtarawala, recalling his war successes so far. Dancers spill onto the stage dancing to local sounds before retreating backstage*).

Narrator: (*Appears on stage*). Yamtarawala's army was emboldened by previous successes on the battlefields, and so they matched onto Miringa with high hopes. The army was reinforced with captured soldiers, and it was an intimidating long stretch of foot soldiers. But, as they attempted to enter Miringa, his military incursion was stopped on its track, just as Galadima had envisaged initially. Yamtarawala found, to his dismay, that Miringa was fortified with a strong Mumba. So the army camped on the outskirts of Miringa, working out plans on how to overrun it.

(Yamtarawala enters the stage with soldiers, looking a bit downcast. The soldiers also lack the regular confidence).

Galadima: Assalamu Alaikum.

All: Wa alaikum assalam.

Galadima: Winners never quit. If you try and do not succeed, try and try again.

Yamtarawala: I am glad we share the same vision. It's not over until it is over.

Galadima: By the way, Miringa didn't surprise me a bit. I knew Mumba was going to constitute an obstacle.

Yamtarawala: You told me earlier what to expect, but warriors like us don't get defeated mentally before we are defeated physically. I don't even think of defeat.

Galadima: But we haven't been defeated. We only suffered a setback. We didn't even encounter an army to fight in the first place. We saw nobody to fight, but we realised that something was impeding our movements.

(The lighting on stage darkens, then switches over to red, showing a flashback scene, a pantomime, where

Yamtarawala's army was struggling to make headway into Miringa, without success. There is no army in sight, but something is impeding their movements. Eventually, they cancel the invasion, out of fear of the unknown, and retreat. In a moment, the scene returns to the present).

Yamtarawala: *(To Galadima and other soldiers).* We have mounted a second charge at Miringa from our forest camp, with little effect. Mumba has refused to let us go into Miringa. I am told it's hidden in a shrine called Tibal, which only the king and a few other people know its location.

Galadima: That's true.

Yamtarawala: Since we have failed to overrun Miringa with our arsenal, we have to find a ploy to unravel the puzzle. I am going to go into the forest as a hunter with a couple of men to see what luck we may find in the Miringa forest. My intuition tells me there may be a way out. There is always a way out if you try.

Galadima: Good idea.

(They leave the stage).

SCENE 2

(*Amid chirps of insects and songs of birds in the forest in the background acoustics, a princess appears on stage with what looks like an aide and a guard, walking casually. The princess is holding a catapult and a sheathed sword tied to her waist*).

Kwatam Gambo: (*Talking to her maid*). Let us rest for a while. We have been wandering for minutes looking for a crested guinea fowl, without luck (*she wipes her face with a hanky*).

Pitum: Princess, I am sure we can find one today if we keep trying (*they sit on a log, resting*).

Kwatam Gambo: It doesn't always take us this long to catch a bird. I think today is a bad day for hunting.

Pitum: A bad day occurs once in a while, but don't conclude yet. Something tells me it's not over yet. Remember the day we caught the white-rumpled swift. We were about to leave the forest when we saw it flying low, and you struck it (*demonstrating*).

Kwatam Gambo: That was a pleasant day to remember. An amazing day, indeed. It also reminds me of the day we caught the first parrot. It just fell on our path on a bad day. Today, each time I see it mimicking my voice, I remember it was a consolation from the heavens.

Kwatam Gambo: I love birds. I keep the beautiful ones in my cages, eat the bigger ones and keep their feathers as memorabilia. I suppose the beautiful colours of the feathers are a fine art by our Maker.

Pitum: My princess, I bow to your hunting skills each time I see the golden eagle in your cage.

Kwatam Gambo: That's one of my best catches ever, and credit goes to me for shooting without killing.

Pitum: I agree with you. It takes a special skill to shoot without missing and to shoot without killing.

Kwatam Gambo: It's an art, and I am the grandmaster.

Pitum: Say it loud. My princess is a hunter with a difference.

Kwatam Gambo: (*Laughs in delight as she stands* up). And I have many birds in this forest to take back to Miringa. If they like, they can hide; but they can't hide forever.

Pitum: My princess is a hunter with a difference.

Kwatam Gambo: Say it again.

Pitum: We have many princesses, but yours is different. Even the forests acknowledge your hunting prowess.

Kwatam Gambo: hahahahaha. The next time I kill a wild goose, you deserve a lap.

Pitum: (*Still praising her*). My princess is a sharpshooter.

Kwatam Gambo: Thank you, Pintu. (*Looking around*). Our voices may be scaring away the birds, don't you think? Let's keep moving in silence (*they stand up, walking stealthily*). We have had enough rest.

Pitum: My princess, your wish is my command. When the princess of Miringa speaks, the raging furnace turns cold all of a sudden.

Kwatam Gambo: Let's keep moving. The leopard moves silently before it pounces and the hyena may not turn up to hunt until the lion has made a big kill.

Pitum: Of course, the lion hides under the savannah grass before it leaps to the sky to take down a gigantic giraffe.

Kwatam Gambo: *(Hushes her and moves stealthily, pointing to a flying bird, and taking a shooting position).* Shhhhh.

Pitum: Oh, it has fled again!

Kwatam Gambo: That sums up a bad day, doesn't it?

Pitum: It's not yet over. Maybe we can go farther into the forest.

Kwatam Gambo: My instinct tells me venturing deeper into the forest is unsafe. There are wild animals lurking in the forest. There are slave raiders from Maiduguri looking for whom to catch and sell to Arabian slave merchants, and there are enemies waiting to strike. The forest isn't always as friendly as it seems, and you know it.

Pitum: My princess, we love the forest and the forest loves us. Let's keep moving.

(*The two ladies and the guard halt their movement on hearing approaching rustles and footsteps. Yamtarawala and his guards walk onto the stage, with games caught in the forest, unaware of the other hunters who have taken shooting positions against them*).

Yamtarawala: (*Startled*). I come in peace (*gesturing to his guards to lower their weapons*). Who are these two beautiful maidens (*ignoring the male guard among them*) in the middle of nowhere? I thought angels lived in heaven. Angels don't walk in the forest, do they?

Kwatam Gambo: Who are you, stranger? Don't move an inch. If you move, we shoot. We aren't joking.

Yamtarawala: (*Pretending to be a commoner, orders his men to surrender*). Lower your swords and guns! These objects are best used against wild animals and humans who behave alike. These ladies should be spared of the scare. (*Introducing himself*). I am Abdullahi the hunter (*shows her some games caught for proof*).

Kwatam Gambo: (*Heaves a sigh of relief, and orders her aide and guard to lower their weapons*). Something about your face tells me you are telling the truth, though you look like an Arabian slave hunter or one from Kanembu area after Lake Chad.

Yamtarawala: *(Laughs aloud)*. I am not a slave hunter. I hunt for animals. I hunt for food. I am of a pure heart. Tell me, what's an angel doing in a lonely forest?

Kwatam Gambo: I can see you are a stranger in this part —who doesn't know Princess Kwatam Gambo of Miringa? Who doesn't know the hunting princess, the boldest of them all?

Yamtarawala: Hu! *(Bows down in reverence)*. I am glad to meet you, princess. I was wondering what an angel looked like until I saw you. You should be resting in the palace while a poor hunter like me hunts on your behalf.

Kwatam Gambo: I wasn't raised to be sitting idle in the palace, waiting for games to come my way. I go after the games myself and adorn the palace with cages and beautiful feathers. I love birds, how they sing merrily, and how they fly in the air effortlessly.

Yamtarawala: Wonderful! How lucky I am to come across a beautiful angel with the heart of a lion. You remind me of the Queen of Sheba.

Kwatam Gambo: Do not flatter me, stranger. I don't need to be reminded that I am made of steel.

Yamtarawalawa: You deserve our respect. Poor Abdullahi has met a super woman in the forest. How blessed is Miringa to have you. Tell me, princess, how far is Miringa from here?

Kwatam Gambo: A bit far, but not as far as going to the Mandara Mountains.

Yamtarawala: And you took the risk to come all the way to the forest? Princess, permit me to hunt for you. Angels do not hunt in the forest alone.

Kwatam Gambo: Thank you for the offer, but I reject your proposal. I am not alone. I am in good company (*pointing to Pitum and the guard*).

Yamtarawala: If you reject my proposal to hunt for your love, please, accept these birds as a special gift from me (*handing her two birds*).

Kwatam Gambo: Stranger, you mean well for me, but you need these birds more than I do. I don't lack food at home; I only hunt for fun. You are a hunter who needs these birds for sustenance. Take them to your family. I am sure they will celebrate with you.

Yamtarawala: From the bottom of my heart, I plead for the princess to accept these games. We are people of the forest; we can hunt all day for new games. Please, accept these gifts (*kneeling down in reverence*).

Maid: (*Whispering to the princess*). Do not turn these birds down. The man appears well-intentioned.

Kwatam Gambo: (*To Yamtarawala*). I like your kind heart, stranger. I will accept the birds. I have had a bad day hunting in the forest. May God grant you your desire for giving me your only catches.

Yamtarawala: Thank you, princess. I hope to see you again.

Kwatam Gambo: I hope, too. I come this way once in a while. By chance, we might see each other again, and it would be my own turn to return your kind gesture. Thank you very much.

Yamtarawala: Thank you, virtuous woman (*waves goodbye as he departs with his team*).

Pitum: (*To Princess*). That's a handsome hunter and one that radiates positive energy. My princess, this man doesn't look bad at all.

Kwatam Gambo: He has a good heart, I can see. He made our day. (*To her maid*). But our day is far spent in the forest already. It's time to go back home. Let's go (*they leave the stage*).

SCENE 3

(The chirps of insects resonate in the background acoustics, mixed with flaps of feathers and rustles of leaves. Yamtarawa appears on stage alone, pacing up and down before embarking on a soliloquy).

Yamtarawala: I won't quit. Yamta the great doesn't lose. Yamta the great doesn't give in when he knows the gains outweigh the risks. It has been two weeks since I met the charming princess. Since then, I have been in this forest four times searching for her, but I haven't been so lucky. The hunting princess has disappeared into thin air, like an eagle vanishing before our very eyes. She showed me how mighty she was, and her memories keep haunting me. I keep imagining how her collection of fathers would look like, with my hands stroking them. Oh princess, come back!

Galadima: (*Walking in*). I can see someone has fallen in love with a lady you are not sure of seeing again. Who knows if she is a spirit?

Yamtarawala: *(Laughs)*. I know she isn't. By the way, warriors don't easily fall in love, for we watch our backs every time, not knowing what love may bring: harmony or disaster. Some of the greatest men in history have been deceived by love. Some have been killed by love. But when I see an angel, I don't need to be told I have come across one. The princess of Miringa has what Yamtarawala cherishes. I cherished that first moment. Who knows, I may cherish many moments.

Galadima: There seems to me more than meets the eye in this profession of love. Your words are profuse and have certain lure about it. Perhaps the spell of an alluring princess could be the real spell we need as a counter force.

Yamtarawala: Allow me to win her heart first before talking about a spell. The hunting princess has eyes that glint like a star and her gait, when she walks, creates more beauty around her slender waist.

Galadima: My oh mine! Yamtarawala is about to give up on our push for Miringa and the ultimate prize for the sake of a beautiful angel. Love, why? Love, why? Love, what have you done to Yamta the great? We have been planning how to take Miringa, and my leader is here singing a love ballad. Love, please, go away and let the valour of Yamtarawala return.

Yamtarawala: (*Laughs*). Galadima, you have known me for a long time. I am not a slave to love, for I know what it means. You know what happened at Mandaragua with the princess. But allow me to win the heart of the hunting princess. I am hunting beyond her heart, as you ought to know by now.

Galadima: I got the whiff of your intention from a distance. I can smell it. Yes, a lover's intent varies with circumstances and —

(*Rustles of leaves and voices are heard as the princess of Miringa, Kwatam Gambo, and her aide appear on stage with their hunting paraphernalia*).

Kwatam Gambo: Who am I seeing?

Yamtararawala: I am Abdullahi the hunter, of course; the one who surrendered his precious birds for the most beautiful princess on earth.

Kwatam Gambo: Please, don't flatter me *(laughs)*. Nice to see you again.

Yamtarawala: A while ago, I was fantasising about you. Just then, you appeared from nowhere, like a long anticipated March rain on a scorching day.

Kwatam Gambo: How has it been?

Yamtarawala: I am grateful to Allah who has kept us alive. That's the most important thing in life.

Kwatam Gambo: What about your family?

Yamtarawala: I am an orphan child. My parents died when I was young, leaving me behind as the only child. But we thank Allah for his mercies.

Kwatam Gambo: Sorry about that (*consoles him with a pat on the back*). They must be proud of the great hunter you have become.

Yamtarawala: Thank you, my princess. Your words are as soothing as Arabian ointment. Your kind is rare to find. How I wish I would live the rest of my life with you. How I wish there were horses for beggars to ride.

Kwatam Gambo: Don't worry, love will find you soon.

Yamtarawala: But something tells me I have found true love already. Something tells me I have found you. Something also tells me you have found me. Don't you think so, pretty one?

Kwatam Gambo: *(Laughs)*. Tomorrow will tell a better story.

Yamtarawala: *(Tickled)*. Tomorrow may even be here already. I can feel it. You can feel its sensuous touch. I can touch it. You can touch it. We can feel its glow without knowing it's here with us already. When you look deeper, you can see tomorrow right in front of you. I am sure you have seen it now, haven't you?

Kwatam Gambo: *(Laughs)*. You are such a nice, funny man.

Yamtarawala: Truth sometimes is clothed in funny talks. Yes.

Kwatam Gambo: Okay, my dear.

Yamtarawala: *(Excited)*. You called me 'my dear'. I am overjoyed *(jumping up and down)*.

Kwatam Gambo: Aren't you one?

Yamtarawala: Insha Allah! Insha Allah!

Narrator: Love is in the air. Kwatam Gambo has fallen for the calculating Yamtarawala. She invited him to the palace, and he honoured her invitation. He never mentioned anything from his Ngazargamu royal background. He disguised himself as just a hunter from nowhere trying to survive in a wicked world, with no parents to cater for.

The ruler of Miringa was moved by his hard luck story and impressed by his hunting prowess. For his lovely daughter to fall in love with a stranger, the king thought the man wasn't an ordinary person, despite that he had no privileges. He, thus, respected his daughter's wishes.

Hence, Yamtarawala ceased to be a forest man momentarily. The king offered him a house in Miringa, where he moved in with a few of his warriors whom he disguised as family members. The rest of the army remained at their temporary location, waiting for a signal.

All the while, Kwatam Gambo never knew Yamtarawala was his father's enemy. Her father, too, didn't know that his enemy was living right under his roof. Yamtarawala expressed interest in marrying Kwatam Gambo, but she didn't say yes immediately.

As their relationship blossomed, Yamtarawala craftily asked her to disclose the secret of Mumba. Kwatam Gambo was a princess given to tradition and etiquettes, and she refused to divulge the secret of Mumba or its location. Yamtarawala was a crafty man, and didn't want to quit trying. He started studying her mannerism: the princess was a habitual beer drinker. She loved the local brew. Yamtarawala had seen a flaw to exploit.

One day, he invited her to his place and offered her so much beer. Princess Kwatam Gambo didn't know when she revealed all the details about the shrine, Tibal, which housed the dreaded Mumba. She also revealed the sacrifice one needed to make before approaching it.

With that information, Yamtarawala offered the required sacrifice and went to the shrine, tearing it down and destroying its potency.

(As the Narrator pauses, the stage lighting ushers in a scene where Yamtarawala is offering a sacrifice to the Tibal, after which he enters and begins to destroy the shrine.

In a bid to send fear into the chief of Miringa and his people, Yamtarawala takes some wrecked pieces of the shrine to the chief, who is now seated at the far end of the stage, with a few loyalists around him.

When the chief and his people see what is in Yamtarawala's possession, they are startled, knowing instantly that the game is over. Their fright makes it impossible for them to fight back, because nobody has succeeded in destroying the Mumba before now. Thus, the chief and Miringa people surrender, and Yamtarawala is seen sitting on his royal seat with authority).

Narrator: Yamtarawala went on to attack surrounding villages, including Gur and Buratai, and conquered all. He was to establish a rule over these conquered territories, but he wasn't satisfied yet, for he knew he hadn't reached his final destination yet. There was still an obstacle on the way.

(*Fade out*).

SCENE 1

(*The palanquin bearers appear on stage carrying Yamtarawala, who is wearing a complacent smile and a reinforced tunic. He paces up and down the stage, talking to himself with gaiety*).

Yamtarawala: I am Yamta the great, who, as a little boy, beheaded fearsome lions, unaided. There is no limit to my guiles and power. What I can't get with my strength, I use my head to get it with ease. I fear no foe.

When some people tried to scare me away with talks of the invisible Mumba, I told them Yamtarawala wasn't a quitter, and so the story ended in my favour. Tibal is no more, and I am the king of Miringa. Gur and Buratai have fallen in line. I am living my dream, no doubt (*laughs hysterically*).

When I left Ngazargamu, I promised that my name would resonate, engraved in gold; and it's happening already. Miringa presented Mumba, and Yamtarawala presented a bait in Kwatam Gambo, the pretty, drunk princess, who helped me to conquer Miringa. Which settlement is next to fall? Which community is standing in Yamtarawala's way? (*Galadima enters the stage*).

Galadima: (*Hailing Yamtarawala*). Yamta the great!

Yamtarawala (*Raises his shoulders high*). Oh yes.

Galadima: Yamta the warrior!

Yamtarawala: (*Dances a little to the right, a little to the left*). Oh yes.

Galadima: Yamta the conqueror of Mumba.

Yamtarawala: (*Repeats the dance*). Oh yes.

Galadima: You have entered the records as a one valiant commander we haven't seen of his kind in the history of Kanem-Bornu.

Yamtarawala: Thank you, Galadima, my dependable ally.

Galadima: Who would have thought Miringa would have been a walkover? I didn't see it coming, to be honest. Mumba was presented as one of the greatest charms ever made by man, but you made a walkover of it, without a fight. The people surrendered, terrified (*shrugs his shoulders*). Of course, it's only Yamtarawala who could do that. Yamtarawala, you are the greatest!

Yamtarawala: Thank you so much. I am delighted to have you as a worthy ally. Without you also, we couldn't have come this far. There would be no rain if there was no sky. There would be no corn if there was no soil. I am glad you believed in me from the beginning. Together, we are making history. Together, we are getting to that great land – the land of milk and honey.

Galadima: Insha Allah.

Yamtarawala: Galadima, but you haven't answered my question – which is the next community to fall?

Galadima: Diwar stands in our way.

Yamtarawala: How strong is Diwar?

Galadima: In terms of a strong fighting force, no army in this part can rival the great Yamtarawala's army, but –

Yamtarawala: But, what?

Galadima: But (*hedges to speak*), but —

Yamtarawala: Speak, Galadima. Speak. Yamtarawala fears no foe.

Galadima: We have done our investigations, and Diwa has its own secret juju behind its military might, which nobody knows its location.

Yamtarawala: (*Turns around sharply*). Here we go again. All these rustic people have different charms to ward off adversaries, but Yamtarawala is no longer fazed by all this. They fall as they come. Galadima, prepare for war in the next few days with Diwar.

Galadima: Your wish is my command.

(*Fade out*).

SCENE 2

Narrator: The battle of Diwar was perhaps the hardest of Yamtarawala's campaigns so far. Though the strength of his army had increased, he was unable to overpower Diwar easily. He tried several times, but there was no headway. Just as Galadima had earlier informed Yamtarawala, the area was strongly fortified spiritually against inversion.

(Yamtarawala and his army appear on stage from the left side. On the right side are the opposing army of Diwar. A real-life, war situation is recreated on stage as the two armies clash for about five minutes. Yamtarawala and his men discover that whatever they throw at the enemy fails to penetrate. At last, they are forced to retreat.

The soldiers vacate the stage with a fade out as Yamtarawala returns to the stage alone, well dressed).

Yamtarawala: Diwar is proving stubborn to fall, but we have a panacea to every stubborn cow – you flog it. I can't get this far in my charge and be slowed down by Diwar. Miringa tried to be stubborn, but I made a walkover of it. I am also told the village chief of Diwar has a beautiful daughter *(laughs)*. Yamtarawala is the master of intrigues *(laughs again)*.

I have to try my luck to unlock the secret of Diwar's resilience. And which pretty lady can see Yamtarawala's face and resist him? *(Turning to the audience)*. Am I not handsome? We all know ladies can be naive when it comes to a handsome man like Yamtarawala. It's not their fault. Yamtarawala is well moulded from the womb by the greatest blacksmith –Allah.

(Admiring himself). I am a hunter. I hunt for food. I hunt for games. I hunt for enemies, I also hunt for beautiful ladies, especially ones who can help further my cause. The Yamtarawala cause is a noble cause. I love women. *(Galadima enters the stage)*.

Galadima *(Teasing)*. Where is Yamtarawala going this early morning, well dressed, on the road to Diwar, unarmed? I suspect something has caught your fancy *(smiles)*. Such an elegant appearance doesn't happen all the time. When a soldier looks this gentle and harmless, I suspect love is in the air, isn't it? Please, explain this chivalrousness.

Yamtarawala: You may not be far from the truth. A brave warrior doesn't only conquer men; he also conquers the hearts of damsels. Looking at the faces of these damsels, he is inspired to conquer enemies, for he doesn't wish to leave them behind for any leering or randy man.

Galadima: What intrigues do you have up your sleeve this time?

Yamtarawala: When Yamtarawala throws his spear into the air, a game falls down with a loud report. When Yamtarawala hunts for damsels, they fall into his arms. This grace is uncommon. It's only given to a special species.

Galadima: I know it. I know this smart dress is like an arrow meant for the heart of an unsuspecting lady.

Yamtarawala: But I am not aiming to kill a game this time. I am, rather, aiming to steal a heart (*both laugh*).

Galadima: Who this time?

Yamtarawala: Your guess is as good as mine.

Galadima: Hmm. I have an idea who she is. I wish you all the best.

Yamtarawala: Trust me, I won't fail you.

(*Galadima leaves the stage. Yamtarawala admires himself once more*).

Yamtarawala: I am like a trap set by a hunter in between two solid stones. A game won't avoid the trap, for the alternative is a longer route. When Yamtarawala sets a trap, it catches before long. It may not be instantly, but games don't ever avoid my traps. Look, I am always enchanted by the perfume of a princess!

(*Yamtarawala begins to walk down the road to Diwar, talking to himself*).

I am also charmed by what I see on the road. The songs of the bird delight me. The rocks amaze me with how they lap on each other. The trees stand at ease, unmoved by a strong wind, even as the leaves on the branches sway violently to the rhythm of the wind. The bleating goats and the strolling fowls add sounds and colours to the workaday life. Life is beautiful.

(Yamtarawala slows down as he notices a lady drawing water from the well).

Which charming lady is hurting her waist to draw water from the well? Can I be of help *(Yamtarawala moves to help out).*

Lady: Thank you, stranger.

Yamta: I want to help you, please.

Lady: Thanks for your offer, but, in Diwar, we are taught to fetch water at a young age. Men have their roles to play and women have their roles. I won't exchange my role for yours, sorry.

Yamtarawala: I am delighted at your resilience. It gladdens my heart that there is one charming lady out there who doesn't want to rest a bit while a good man relieves her of stress. Such a woman is the kind we all ask for in a man's house to raise his future children.

Jaina: *(Shyly).* Thanks for the compliments.

Yamtarawala: Tell me, pretty one, what's your name?

Jaina: I am Jaina.

Yamtarawala: What a lovely name, Jaina. It makes someone smack his lips after pronouncing the sweet sounding name.

Jaina: Thank you, stranger.

Yamtarawala: Whose daughter are you? Are you the daughter of the great Diwar king?

Jaina: No, I am just a slave at the chief's palace.

Yamtarawala: Your status doesn't diminish your appeal to me, nevertheless. It doesn't change my admiration for you either. You see, many dream of sleeping in the courtyard of the chief for just one night, but you are already living there. Can you take me to the princess? You even look like a princess.

Lady: *(Tickled)*. Thank you very much. It's my pleasure. Where are you from?

Yamtarawala: I am from the village after Miringa, to the east. Each time I feel bored, I take a walk to this part for a breath of fresh air. There is something about Diwar that's seductive. I don't know exactly what, but Diwar has cast a spell on me.

Lady: You speak eloquently like a noble, are you one?

Yamtarawala: Unfortunately, I am not; but the ways of nobility impress me. It delights me like *fura da nono* put into your mouth on a hot afternoon.

Lady: Thank you so much. But I am not sure the princess would welcome the idea.

Yamtarawala: I admire everything you do, including how you try to protect the princess' privacy. I like that. But who doesn't like seeing the *fur kamda shishi* (the fig tree) in their compound? Is there anybody who doesn't like the towering *fur kwagu* (baobab tree) in their compound? I don't like blowing my trumpet, but I sprout like the fig and baobab trees wherever I go. I am —

(*The princess walks onto the stage, surprised to see her slave conversing with a man*).

Princess: (*To Jaina*). This is getting interesting; my girl seems to have fallen in love with fur kamda shishi and fur kwagu *(laughs)*.

Yamtarawala: (*Roars with laughter*). Don't accuse the innocent girl, she hasn't fallen in love with anybody.

Princess: But I overheard her talking with you, or didn't I?

Yamtarawala: We did talk, but our conversation had nothing to do with falling in love or out of it.

Princess: So, how did the fig tree and baobab tree analogies creep into your idle discussion?

Yamtarawala: I was merely asking her to take me to the princess to tell her she has done well in raising her to become a decent girl. Nothing more.

Princess: Is that so?

Yamtarawala: Nothing else.

Princess: By the way, who are you?

Yamtarawala: I am Abdullahi the hunter.

Princess (*Runs her eyes all over him*). You look too decent to be a hunter, do hunters dress like gentlemen? I can't see you with any weapon.

Yamtarawala: Hunters do not live one-dimensional life in the forest. Like any other person, we also lead a normal life. I am not a stereotype. I lend myself to many possibilities.

Princess: (*Nodding her head*). Quite interesting.

Yamtarawala: Can you take me to the princess of Diwar? I would like to meet her.

Princess: What would you like the princess to do for you?

Yamtarawala: I have already hinted to you a while ago about my intention –to commend her for the good work she has done in this life of this decent lady.

Princess: Is that all?

Yamtarawala: For now, that's all.

Princess of Diwar: If that is the case, your message has already been delivered to the princess of Diwar.

Yamtarawala: How?

Princess of Diwar: When the drum sounds from the palace of the chief, its echoes travel to the inner recesses of the soul far away. The wind is a dedicated messenger.

Yamtarawala: But it's not in every situation, my dear. Mountains can intercept the journey of the windy messenger.

Princess of Diwar: I think I have made myself clear that the princess of Diwar has received your message.

Yamtarawala: (*Eyes glazing*). Are you the princess of Diwar?

Princess of Diwar: I didn't speak in riddles. Riddles are the language of the elders and the noble.

Yamtarawala: How honoured I am to stand in the presence of the princess of Diwar. Your fame precedes your age.

Princess of Diwar: Don't flatter me, please. You are the real fur kamda shishi and the fur kwagu. I am neither of these. I am just ordinary.

Yamtarawala: Can a sunflower be ordinary? This lie doesn't fit you at all. You may undervalue your real worth, but everybody who sees you knows you are the opposite of what you claim. All of us hear about you. You are worth more than gold.

Princess of Diwar: I have never heard so much flattery in one day since I was born than I have heard from you. Thank you very much, stranger. You tend to make me feel important, but I won't get carried away by how sweet your words sound. I won't.

Yamtarawala: Your humility is self-evident, and I am not surprised you don't want to acknowledge the obvious.

Princess of Diwar: There you go again.

Yamtarawala: If I had my way, I would have loved to be your hunter, go into the wild, and deliver the best games, even lions. Hope I am not asking for too much?

Princess of Diwar: I don't know. I don't really know. Can you, please, allow us to take our leave now?

Yamtarawala: Who am I to stop you from taking your leave? But this leave would be more honourable if you save me from dying.

Princess of Diwar: Dying? How?

Yamtarawala: Yes. If you reject my offer, I may put a dagger to my skull or strike my head on a stone. Your charms have taken over my senses. I can't think of anything else apart from you now. Please, help me.

Princess of Diwar: (*In awe*). Please, don't do anything funny (*hugging him*). I will think about your offer. Can I take my leave now?

Yamtarawala: Yes, you can (*leading her offstage, holding her left hand with his right hand*).

Narrator: The chief's daughter merely pretended to play hard-to-get for a while. Yamtarawala was too irresistible for her. Taking advantage of her feelings, Yamtarawala seduced her. She allowed him to stay with her late in the night.

By midnight, when everybody had slept, the chief's daughter took him to where her father kept his spear, on Yamtarawala's request. She bragged to him that no army could overpower Diwar as long as her father was in possession of the magical spear. Armed with that secret, Yamtarawala thanked her and departed Diwar.

Yamtarawala went back to his army and began to plot how to work on the Diwar secret. He decided to visit Diwar on the day of harvest when he knew that most people living with the chief had gone to the farm to harvest corn for him and the daughter would probably remain behind. It worked.

The chief's daughter offered him a drink. She loved drinking, too, and she even got herself drunk. Yamtarawala wasn't actually after her love, so he killed her in cold blood, escaped with her father's spear and left the scene.

Three days after the death of the king's daughter, he returned to Diwar with his army in full strength, and defeated it, just as he did to Miringa. With mission accomplished, he settled in the Biu area and overthrew the traditional setup to establish a new dynasty.

(A battle scene appears on stage immediately as the Narrator ends his thread of narrative. Yamtarawala and his army appear fighting with the Miringa army. Outnumbering the opposition, they are all over them, shooting and killing with swords and daggers. Yamtarawala, dressed in reinforced tunic and fighting with body armour, cuts off the head of the leader of the Miringa army, holding it aloof. The remainder of the vanquished army take to their heels. Fade out).

SCENE 1

(1535. The stage is full of armed royal warriors, men and women discussing in clusters while waiting for the address of Yamtarawala, the king. Soon, the palanquin bearers appear on stage carrying Yamtarawala, who acknowledges cheers from the crowd. Dressed in a king's regalia, Yamtarawala is wearing a red fez cap and a blue pigtail titled to the right, completely covered with white turban. His sons are dressed like princes, wearing a red fez cap, with no pigtail, over white turban.

Kingmakers are dressed in red fez caps, with no pigtail and any turban. Yamtarawala alights from the palanquin, takes ponderous footsteps as he sits down on a golden, royal throne. Silence falls).

Yamtarawala: I greet you all (*he raises his clenched right fist to his chest. Others respond the same way*). This is a day of joy. It has been a long journey, but we made it at long last. It has been a tortuous journey from Ngazargamu –a journey that has claimed many lives, both men and women, including children. It has taken us many years to get to this great land. We believed. We fought hard, and we triumphed. It is not by our might but the will of God. Allahu Akbar.

I want to thank everybody who made it to this land, just as I commiserate with those who died valiantly. Your sacrifices and theirs will ever remain deathless.

Yesterday, Kingmakers made me a king. It was the culmination of a dream I nursed many years ago. When we left Ngazargamu, I told my detractors with pride, "Youman teram wallahianasultan, insha Allah. Yau ma tara wal."

You know what that means – "One day, you will see I am a chief. We will see each other again." Today, I am a chief, your chief (*plaudits reverberate as the Chorus sings his praise*). The first prophecy has come to pass. And, one day, Ngazargamu will see me again as a royalty, not as a forsaken prince. My empire-seeking adventure has ended with the formation of this new empire. What a beautiful place we have inherited with escarpments dotting the environment. Visit

Viukuthla, and you will find plenty of games to hunt for fun. We are blessed.

From today, we shall be the envy of Ngazargamu, Bulala, Ashanti, Songhay, Ethiopia, Egypt, Syria, Dahomey, Morocco and other great empires on the face of the earth. Rejoice with me. Dance to Bansuwe. Sing and jump about. Dance to Waksha Washa and Mwar Mwari. Thank you. Thank you.

You are all witnesses to history –the history of Yamtarawala and the new empire. I have set an empire no power on earth can easily overrun. The dominion of our empire stretches from River Gongola to Kopchi, more than 5,000 square miles. This is a major feat, my people.

(The trumpet sounds as celebration begins).

Narrator: Yamtarawala means Yamta the great. As you can see, this is the story of a great warrior, who was schemed out of the kingship of the Kanem-Bornu Empire and the Ngazargamu palace as the first son. He didn't stay behind to fight his detractors, but he took 72 men from Ngazargamu and headed for the Mandara Mountains to begin an empire-seeking adventure that lasted many years. He came across many tribulations, but he never cowered.

After his coronation as the Kuthli (King) of Biu, he ruled over the vast territory with his sons and followers outside the influence of Ngazargamu. In his journey from Ngazargamu to Biu area, Yamtarawala has acquired great mystical powers. He felt secure, for he thought nobody else had higher powers. His only fear was his children, whom he felt might know what he knew. So he became suspicious of them.

SCENE 2

(*Yamtarawala is seated on the throne, regally dressed and surrounded by royal warriors. Four mats are placed on the floor in a square form about two and half feet from his legs. He puts a stone inside a clay pot, pours water inside it, and begins to boil it*).

Yamtarawala: (*To one of his guards*). I want you to fetch my sons –Marivirahyel, Pachang, Diriwala and Pihtum– and my daughters – Purkwa and Awa – immediately.

Guard 1: (Bowing down). Yes, Your Highness (*he leaves the palace*).

Yamtarawala: (*Soliloquising*). Yamtarawala can't be rivalled in my kingdom by any man born of a woman. I don't care whether they are my own children or strangers. From my experiences in Miringa and Diwar, the downfall of a man begins from his home. It takes a stranger quite some time to penetrate the inner recesses of your abode, but it takes your family members no time to undo what you have gained overtime. I don't want it to happen in my lifetime. I don't want to leave anything to chance.

(*Guard 1 appears with his six children, looking anxious but not terrified*).

Guard 1: (*To Yamtarawala*). They are here, Your Highness.

Yamtarawala: (*Gestures them to sit on the mat after acknowledging greetings*). You are all welcome (*silence falls for a moment, and his gazes at each face*). How strong you are is also determined by how strong your children are. That's why I have called you today to find how smart and strong each of you is. I want to perform a simple test to find out if you are following in the footsteps of your father, or you are just like a pebble which, when tossed into the air, falls down on the ground and never rises again (*his children giggle*).

Now, I want each person to come forward. You are going to use this stick to find out if the stone in the boiling pot has cooked and become soft.

All: (*Looking aghast and murmuring*) How can a cooked stone become soft?

Yamtarawala: (*To the first daughter*). Purkwa, it's your turn to check if the stone has cooked. I have been cooking it for minutes now.

Purkwa: (*Takes a few steps, collects the stick from his father, opens the pot, steers the boiling stone, and shakes her head*). The stone is yet to be cooked).

Yamtarawala: Alright. Please, hand over the stick to your sister (*she obeys*).

Awa: (*Takes a few steps, opens the pot, and steers the boiling stone. Shakes her head as she closes the pot*). The stone is yet to be cooked.

Yamtarawala: It's okay. It's okay. Please, hand over the stick to your brother, Pihtum, for his own test.

Pihtum: (*Takes a few footsteps, steers the boiling stone, shakes his head and closes the pot*). The stone is yet to be cooked.

Yamtarawala: Alright. (*To Pachang*). You can come forward for your test.

Pachang: (*Moves in the direction of the boiling stone after collecting the stick from Pihtum, and steers it*). I am afraid the stone is yet to be cooked.

Yamtarawala: Alright. Please, hand over the stick to your brother, Diriwala, to test the stone.

Diriwala: (*Steps forward, steers the boiling stone, and shakes his head as he closes the pot*). No luck, Your Highness; the stone is yet to be cooked.

Yamtarawala: Alright. Please, hand over the stick to your brother, Marivirahyel, for his own test.

Marivirahyel: (*Steps forward, walks around the boiling pot, dips the stick inside the stone and brings out a soft stone. As he stands in front of his bewildered father, he starts tearing the soft stone with his teeth*). Your Highness, the stone has been cooked.

(*Murmurs of surprise rend the air as everybody exchanges surprising glances*).

Yamtarawala: (*Speaking tongue in cheek*). I am delighted that the son of the lion has rivalled the valour of the greatest animal on earth. Marivirahyel, you have become a man. Well-done. (*To all his children*). You now can take your leave. I am proud of all of you, particularly Marivirahyel.

All: (*In unison*). Thank you, His Highness.

Yamtarawala: (*Soliloquising*). I knew it. I have always suspected Marivirahyel is working behind the scenes to fortify himself to undo me. From today, I can only sleep with one eye open. The reality here is that only somebody who possesses a higher power can make another person's mystical stone become too soft for a stick to pierce into it. I am in trouble. Yamtarawala is in deep trouble.

Narrator: For once in his lifetime, Yamtarawala, the great warrior from the Ngazargamu dynasty, the conqueror of lions and warriors, is panicking, scared of his life, when there is no visible threat to his kingship. Until now, he had cut a larger-than-life figure. Now, courage seems to be deserting him.

Arising from this perceived threat to his throne, Yamtarawala arranged some assailants to kill his son. The assignment was executed, but, unknown to them, Marivirahyel had escaped. Meanwhile, the prince was presumed dead, and was being mourned in the palace.

SCENE 3

(A pantomime: a group of assailants appear on stage in silhouettes with swords and clubs, baying for the blood of Mariyavhel, who runs around the stage, crying for help. The pantomime reveals a sluggish scene when the attackers descend on Marivirahyel, who struggles to fend off the attacks, until he escapes their stranglehold, limping off the stage).

Marivirahyel: (Scene switches over to real-life situation, with him in shock, on a lonely path). It's hard to believe that my own father would go all out to hurt me. I haven't done anything wrong against him for all I know. Fortifying myself against eventuality shouldn't be a crime. I haven't challenged the king to a combat nor have I plotted against his downfall. Why should King Yamtarawala be so insecure that he thinks the only way he could be immortal was to get rid of me? What have I done wrong?

Yamtarawala has conquered men. He has conquered settlements. He has conquered chiefdoms and kingdoms, now he wants to conquer his own family? What has come over the king?

My father should know that, though the lion is the strongest animal in the wild, it never devours its own children, no matter how hungry and angry he may be. King Yamtarawala should stop wasting his time trying to kill me. It won't work. It will never work.

(*He goes into hiding on hearing approaching footsteps. A group of men and women from another village appear on the far end of the stage, discussing the "death" of Marivirayhel, as they trek to the palace to sympathise with the king. But Marivirayhel appears from hiding and addresses them*).

Marivirayhel: Greetings (*raising his right arm and clenched fist towards his chest, according to tradition*).

Strangers 1: I greet you (*making the same fist gesture*).

Stranger 2: Your face looks familiar and your voice sounds familiar.

Stranger 3: (*Whispering to stranger 2*). He looks like Marivirayhel, the dead prince.

Stranger 2: *(Startled)*. Marivirayhel?

Marivirayhel: Calm down, I know what you are whispering to yourselves: you thought I was dead, and you were going to the palace of Yamtarawala to sympathise with the crafty king. Well, I am neither dead nor a ghost. I am still Marivirahyel, the prince. When you get to the palace, please, tell Yamtarawala that, I, his son, Marivirahyel, said that, if he has *nono* (milk), I have *fura* (morsel); and, if he has *taba* (tobacco), I have *klbu* (potash). You heard me well?

Strangers: (*In unison*). You said we should tell the king that, if he had *nono*, you had *fura*; and, if he had *taba*, you had *klibu*.

Marivirahyel: Correct. Now you can go.

(*Strangers leave the stage in a hurry, looking behind their backs, in fear*).

SCENE 4

(*The royal palace. The king sits on the throne, surrounded by the royal warriors and courtiers. Sympathisers can be seen sitting on the mat sympathising with him over the death of his son, Marivirahyel. Some are seen crying, some rolling on the floor, In the background, the Chorus sings a dirge*).

Yamtarawala: (*Rising to speak*). Allah gives and Allah takes. In good times, we praise Allah. In bad times, we also praise Allah. Marivirahyel was one of my sons whom I was proud of. He was everything I desired in a son: witty, fearless and spiritually strong. But whom am I to question the will of Allah? He has gone the way of all mortals. For all of us mourning this great son of the soil, weep no more. My son, Marivirahyel, will –

(*His speech is interrupted by Strangers who enter the stage, panting. He addresses them with urgency*).

Who are these peasants interrupting the Kuthli and panting like disappointed leopards that have failed in their bid to kill a prey? What is after you? A lion or a cobra?

Strangers: (*In unison*). None of the above.

Yamtarawala: Then, what?

Stranger 1: We saw the prince.

Yamtarawala: Which prince?

Stranger 2: The dead prince, Marivirahyel.

Stranger 1: We were coming to the palace to sympathise with you when he appeared from nowhere and spoke to us.

Yamtarawala: You saw a ghost who spoke to you?

Stranger 1: We thought he was a ghost, but when he spoke to us, we realised he was no ghost.

Yamtarawala: (*Walking up to Stranger 1*). What did he say?

Stranger 1: (*Visibly shaken*). He said (*stammering*) … he said we should tell you that, if you had *nono*, he had *fura;* and, if you had *taba*, he had *klibu*.

Yamtarawala: What insolence! This is a public disgrace. In essence, Mariyivarhel is telling me that he is ready to outwit whatever his father, Yamtarawala, has against him. Can you imagine that! Can you imagine the challenge? Under my eyes, a cub weaned under my care, has grown to wrestle with the lion (*pacing about*). No man has issued an open challenge to Yamtarawala, but my own son is challenging an avatar to a wrestling contest (*laughing in derision*) Marivirahyel, your days are numbered!

(*Remembering the strangers are still around, he angrily addresses them*). You bearers of heart-breaking news, get out of my sight! I place a curse on you to remain vagabonds till the end of your lives. Get out of my sight now before I do something terrible to you!

(*The strangers run away, afraid. The sympathisers also sneak away, confused*).

Chorus: (*Singing*):

Yamtarawala has been beaten to his own game

Yamtarawala thought he had the world under his feet

But his feet are beginning to wobble

The Yamtarawala you knew is not the same Yamtarawala of today.

Yamtarawala: (*In a pensive mood, gestures to his guards to leave the stage*). How can I endure this public disgrace? I have been outwitted and ridiculed by my own son. It is finished.

(*He moves back to the throne, sits awkwardly and begins to sink into the ground. Awa, one of his daughters, rushes in, bewildered, raising an alarm that attracts the attention of his mother. Desperate not to lose every part of the sinking king, Queen 2 picks a knife and cuts off his zukumbli – pigtail*).

EPILOGUE

(*The king's courtyard. Locals discuss in hushed tones about the death of Yamtarawala. They wear sorrowful looks but stop short of weeping, for the death isn't officially announced yet. Suddenly, Kingmaker 1 appears on stage wearing a red fez cap and pigtail*).

Kingmaker 1: (*In a loud voice*). *Hyel knthla! Hyel knthla! Hyel knthla!* Heaven has fallen! Heaven has fallen! Heaven has fallen!

(*Cries of anguish rend in the air as locals begin to mourn the passage of the Kuthli*).

Chorus: (*Begins to sing* the *thlimfwal — praise song for the departed*).

Ya kituwa mma kari
Kara thlawarda
Iya iya
Ga
mwarya
Iya Iya.

Too heavy to carry, yet mother is in need of it
Greet them
Iya Iya (chorus)
So you are going
Iya Iya.

Talaka wutuwa
Hyelkarta
Kara thlawarda
Iya iya (chorus)
Ga mwarya
Ga mwarya
Iya iya.

Common man can't get it
It's under God's protection
Greet them
Iya iya (chorus)
So you are going?
Iya iya.

(The palanquin bearers appear on stage, carrying the wrapped body of the dead king, followed by members of the royal family, Kingmakers, royal warriors and locals. They walk slowly, silently around the stage thrice before taking their exit).

(THE END).

ABOUT THE AUTHOR

Henry Akubuiro is one of Nigeria's revered journalists and a multi genre author who navigates the world of letters – prose, drama, poetry and children's literature. Also a biographer, he is the author of the critically acclaimed novel, *Prodigals in Paradise*; the novellas – *Little Wizard of Okokomaiko, Adventures of Bingo and Bomboy,* and *Vershima and the Missing Cow.*

Since 2005, he has been editing the "The Sun Literary Review", regarded as the longest running literary supplement in Nigerian media, where he has functioned as a reviewer, critic and interviewer, providing a platform for Nigerian and African writers to showcase their creative works and air their views about writings.

His reviews, interviews and short stories have appeared in *OPEC magazine*, Austria; *ALA Journal*, USA; *Maple Tree Literary Supplement*, Canada, among others.

Akubuiro is currently an assistant editor with *The Sun* Newspaper, Lagos, one of Nigeria's most popular media brands.

www.ingramcontent.com/pod-product-compliance
Lightning Source LLC
Chambersburg PA
CBHW021112080526
44587CB00010B/496